Inspirations

Illustrations by
Jan Gallehawk

This is the way to live,
that after you
have gone, people will
wish that you were still
around to give them
comfort and counsel,
love, care,
understanding and
concern.

Louise Benes

*God invented the
giving of love, but
he won't mind if
we borrow the idea.*

In the long run,
pessimists may be
proven right,
But the optimist
has a better time on
the trip.

Faith is putting
all your eggs in
God's basket and
counting your
blessings before
they've hatched.

Doubts which are embraced as being the final word are dangerous, while doubts which are seen to be an intermediate step can lead us foreword.

The best tranquilliser is a clear conscience.

Cleanliness may be next to godliness but for a small child it's next to impossible.

Little Boy's Prayer

Dear God, take care of
my family, take care of
the whole world. And
please, God, take care of
Yourself, or we're all
sunk.

The art of
acceptance
is the art of making
someone who has
just
done you a small
favour
wish that they had
done you a greater
one.

We are always in
the forge, or on the
anvil; by trials
God is shaping us
for higher things.

The nature of love
is much more a
doing than a
feeling.

If you awake and see the
sunrise
Bathing earth in red
and gold,
As you gaze you'll
somehow find
It fills one with
anticipation
To start the day with
such a sight.
God is so very good to
give
A fresh new day,
giftwrapped so bright.

Life is an opportunity, benefit from it.
Life is beauty, admire it.
Life is a dream, realise it.
Life is a challenge meet it.
Life is a duty, complete it.
Life is a game, play it.
Life is costly, care for it.
Life is wealth, keep it.
Life is love, enjoy it.
Life is a mystery, know it.
Life is a promise, fulfil it.
Life is sorrow, overcome it.
Life is a song, sing it.
Life is a struggle, accept it.
Life is a tragedy, confront it.
Life is an adventure, dare it.
Life is luck, make it.
Life is too precious, do not destroy it.
Life is life, fight for it.

Mother Teresa.

*Insight is a gift
that comes to those
who hunger after
truth.*

Not to be sure

opens up new

opportunities to

search out the truth.

Keep your temper.
Do not quarrel
with an angry
person, but
give him a soft
answer. It is
commanded by the
Holy Writ and,
further more, it
makes him madder
than anything else
you say.

I am sure we must rise to the great responsibilities which are peculiarly our own, and yet at the same time fulfil the common place tasks of daily life.

*Difficulty is no
barrier to
faith and hope.*

*There is always
time to add a word,
never time to
withdraw one.*

Prayer gives a man the opportunity of getting to know a gentleman he hardly ever meets. Not his maker, but himself.

Make sure it is
God's trumpet you
are blowing —
If it is only yours,
it won't wake the
dead;
It will simply
disturb the
neighbours.

Lost time is when
we learn nothing
from the
experiences of life.

Everyone is in favour of going to heaven, but too many are waiting for the entrance requirements to ease.

Faith makes
The uplook good
The outlook bright,
The inlook favourable,
And the future glorious.

We give love away
- and it becomes the
best part of us.

Give me a mind that is
not bored
That does not whimper,
whine or sigh;
Don't let me worry
overmuch ,   ,
About the fussy thing
called I .
Give me a sense of
humour, Lord,
Give me the grace to see
a joke,
To get some happiness
from life,
And pass it on to other
folk.

Deeds are stronger
than words and
lifestyle must
undergird our
proclamation to
give it meaning
and integrity.

*Prayer changes
things, particularly
the one who prays.*

Brooding over
one's troubles
ensures a perfect
hatch.

Say what you will about the 10 commandments, you always come back to the pleasant fact that there are only 10 of them.

To err is human
To forgive takes
restraint;
To forget you
forgave.
Is the mark of a
saint.

*Sharing multiplies
happiness and
divides sorrow.*

My relationship with God is part of my relationship with man. Failure in one will cause failure with the other.

*Only the one who
hopes has a future.*

*We can only give
what we are and
not what we would
like to be.*

*Happy
Christmas
to our Christian
friends; happy
Chanukah to our
Jewish friends; to
our atheist friends…
good luck!*

An aged grandmother, who never attended school, once gave her grand daughter a slip of paper with all the advice she would ever need to lead a good life. What she wrote is valuable for all of us: Wash what is dirty. Water what is dry. Heal what is wounded. Warm what is cold. Guide what goes off the road. And love people who are the least loveable, because they need it most."

That which we
repeatedly think
about and embrace
as truth will become
an integral part of
our lives.

If you will please people,
you must please them in
their own way;
and as you cannot make
them what they should be,
you must take them as
they are.

May the road rise to
meet you,
May the wind be always
at your back,
May the sunshine warm
upon your face.
May the rain fall soft
upon your fields
and until we meet again.
May God hold you in
the palm of his hand.

Often the things we grasp after as giving us meaning and security are the very things that undermine the fabric of our lives.

*To do business
with an honest
person you must
first be an honest
person.*

GOD'S GIFT OF TIME

Take time to think, it is
the source of power.
Take time to play, it is
the secret of perpetual
youth.
Take time to read, it is
the fountain of wisdom.
Take time to pray, it is
the greatest power on
earth.
Take time to love, to be
loved: it is God's given
privilege.

Take time to laugh, it is
the music of the soul.
Take time to give, it is
too short a day to be
selfish.
Take time to work, it is
the price of success.

*...the cheerful heart
has a continual
feast.*

God does everything for a reason. He made you to do special things for him... Many things that you, and only you can do. You are a bond between people. You influence their lives. Whether you're happy, sick or suffering all these things are for God.

May the Lord help you realise why he made you. Let your life bring joy, patience and love to others.

Too many God's,
so many creeds,
Too many paths
that wind and
wind,
When just the art
of being kind
Is all the sad
world needs.

Don't be afraid to take big steps. You can't cross a chasm in two small steps.

*I'm not going to worry
Unless the animals start
lining up
two by two for the next
space shuttle!*

To know that
others have walked
a similar road may
not make the
difficulties of the
journey easier, but
should give us hope.

In my sleep he
watches yearning
and restores my
soul,
so that each
recurring morning,
love and goodness
make me whole.

*To pass something
on to another is not
to lose it but to
invest it.*

What are we in ourselves, and what we owe to others, makes us a complete whole.

Caring is a beautiful
word. It is a mother's
arms:
a father's affection
a drooping posy of wild-
flowers proffered by a
sticky small hand.
It is a grandma's
understanding: the smile
in a voice on the
telephone: a letter from
an old friend:
apple pie baked by a
neighbour for a house-
wife who is not well.

Most of us can afford to take a
lesson from the oyster.

The irritations get into his shell.
He doesn't like them.
But he can't get rid of them, so
he settles down to make of them
one of the most beautiful things
in the world;
he makes his irritations into a
lovely pearl.
There are irritations in our
lives today,
And there is only one
prescription, make a pearl.
It may have to be a pearl of
patience,
But anyhow make a pearl.
It takes faith and love to do it.

We can have a full
life even when we
haven't got
everything we
want.

*True peace is not
an uneasy truce;
it is the fruit of
genuine openness
and forgiveness.*

Difficulty is not outside of God's design for our lives, but God is never inside the difficulty unless we put him there.

It is -
a welcoming floppy-eared
dog:
a compassionate word for
a sorrowing heart.
It is - room in
somebody's lap when a
child is small and room in
somebody's heart when a
man is very old.
Caring is a beautiful
word.
It is akin to love.

*We should not
have expectations of
others regarding
things that we are
not prepared to
carry out ourselves.*

In ordinary life we hardly realise that we receive a great deal more than we give, and it is only with gratitude that life becomes rich.
It is very easy to over-estimate the importance of our own achievements in comparison with what we owe others.